VOCAL SHEET MUSIC

MEN'S EDITION

SINGER + PIANO/GUITAR

BROADWAY FAVORITES

ISBN 978-1-5400-1521-1

HAL•LEONARD®

Visit Hal Leonard Online at
www.halleonard.com

Contact Us:
Hal Leonard
7777 West Bluemound Road
Milwaukee, WI 53213
Email: info@halleonard.com

In Europe contact:
Hal Leonard Europe Limited
42 Wigmore Street
Marylebone, London, W1U 2RN
Email: info@halleonardeurope.com

In Australia contact:
Hal Leonard Australia Pty. Ltd.
4 Lentara Court
Cheltenham, Victoria, 3192 Australia
Email: info@halleonard.com.au

ALL THAT'S KNOWN
from SPRING AWAKENING

Lyrics by STEVEN SATER
Music by DUNCAN SHEIK

FOR FOREVER
from DEAR EVAN HANSEN

Music and Lyrics by BENJ PASEK
and JUSTIN PAUL
Vocal arrangements by Justin Paul
Piano arrangement by
Alex Lacamoire and Justin Paul

EVAN: *conversationally*

End of May, or ear-ly June __ This pic-ture-per-fect af-ter-noon __ we __ share

Drive the wind-ing coun-try road __ Grab a scoop at "A La Mode" __ and then... we're there

With pedal

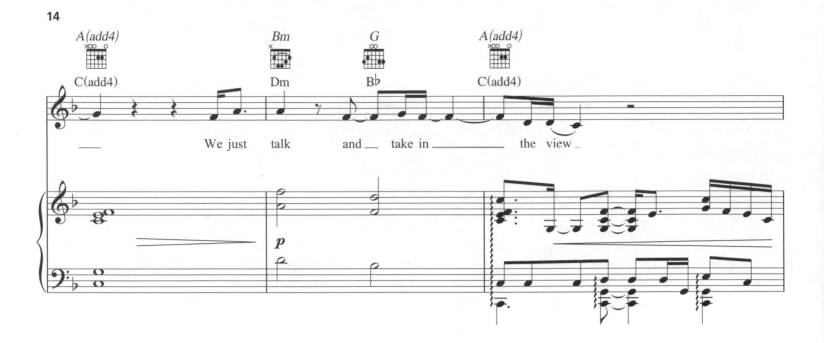

We just talk and __ take in _____ the view __

Hold back (♩ = 96)

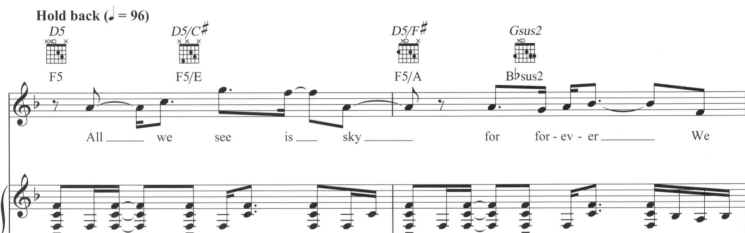

All _____ we see is __ sky _____ for for - ev - er _____ We

let _____ the world pass _ by _____ for for - ev - er _____

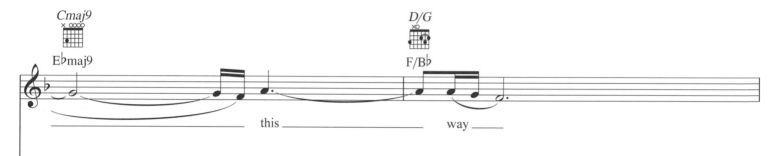

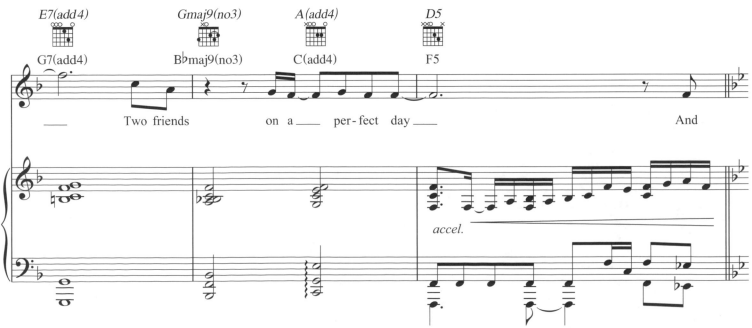

Picking up speed (♩ = 100)

One foot af - ter the oth - er   One branch then __ to an - oth - er

I climb high - er and high - er   I climb 'til __ the en - tire __

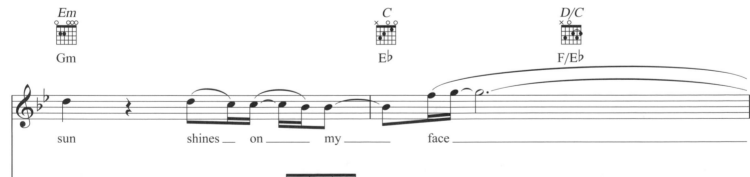

sun   shines __ on _____ my _____ face _____

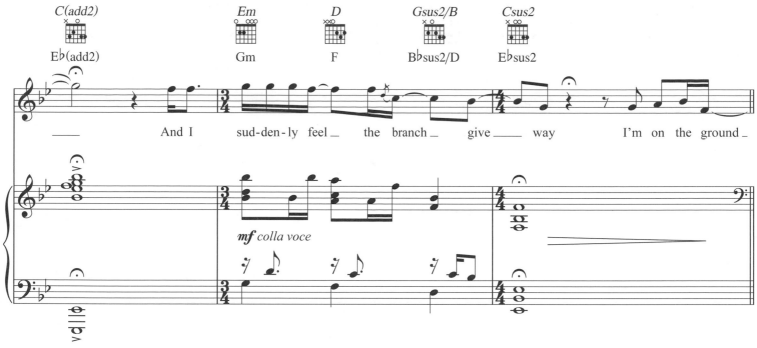

And I sud-den-ly feel __ the branch __ give __ way I'm on the ground __

Slower

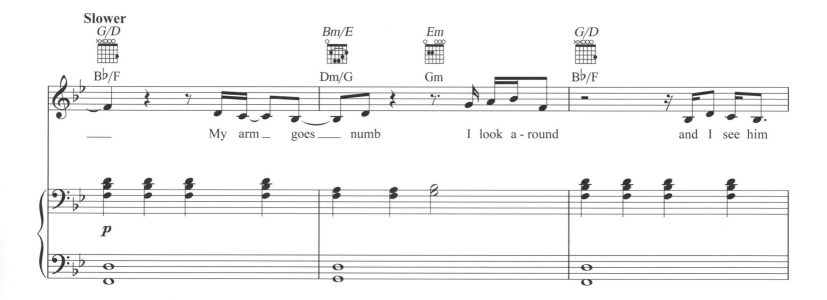

__ My arm __ goes __ numb I look a - round and I see him

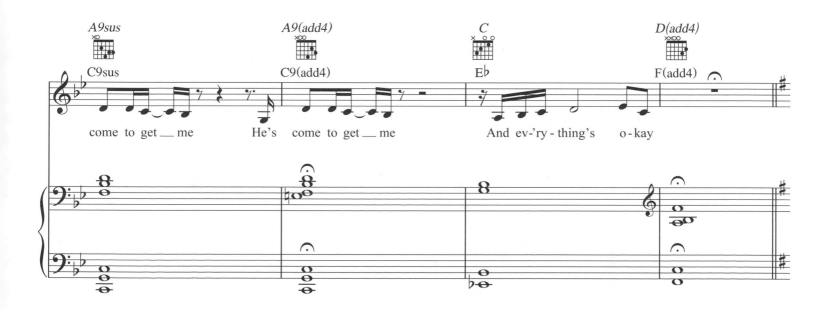

come to get __ me He's come to get __ me And ev-'ry-thing's o-kay

FIGHT THE DRAGONS
from BIG FISH

Music and Lyrics by
ANDREW LIPPA

I've nev-er been a man__ who lived__ an of-fice life.

I've nev-er been a man__ be-hind__ a desk.

I've al-ways been a man__ who said__ that

stay-in' still __ is play-in' dead, __ the kind who's look-in' for-ward to __ the

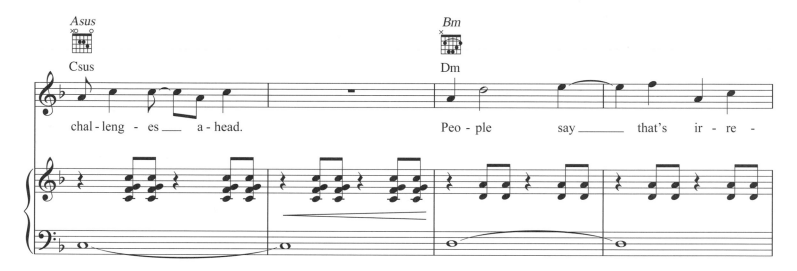

chal-leng-es __ a-head. Peo-ple say __ that's ir-re-

spon-si-ble. __ Peo-ple tell __ me, "Stay at

home." But I'm not __ made __ for things like

FORTUNE FAVORS THE BRAVE

from AIDA

Music by ELTON JOHN
Lyrics by TIM RICE

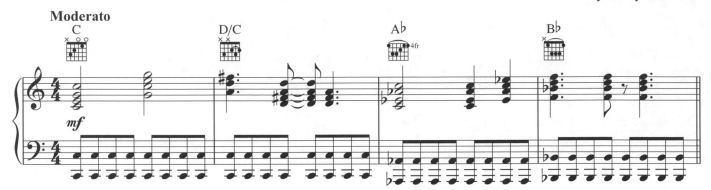

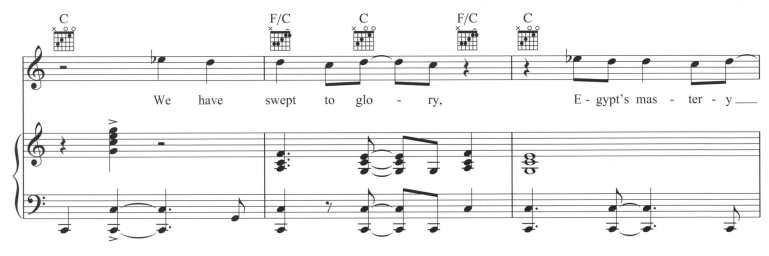

We have swept to glo - ry, E - gypt's mas - ter - y____

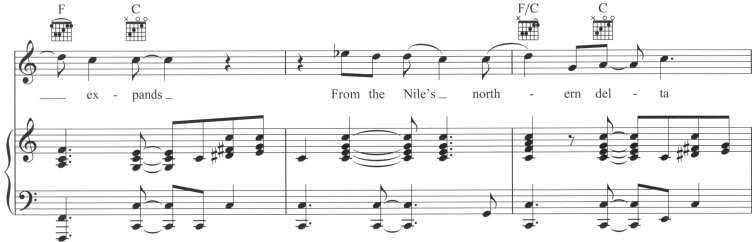

____ ex - pands ____ From the Nile's ____ north - ern del - ta

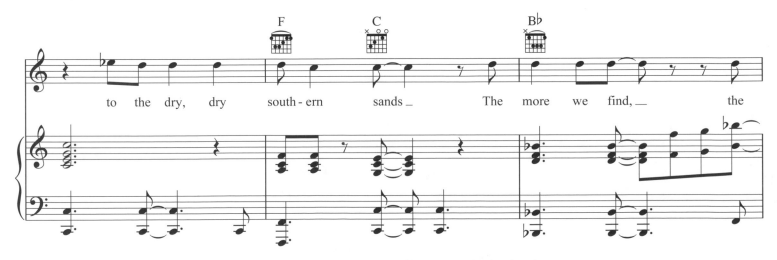

to the dry, dry south - ern sands ____ The more we find, ____ the

more we see, ___ the more ___ we come ___ to learn ___ The more that

we ex - plore, ___ the more ___ we shall re - turn ___

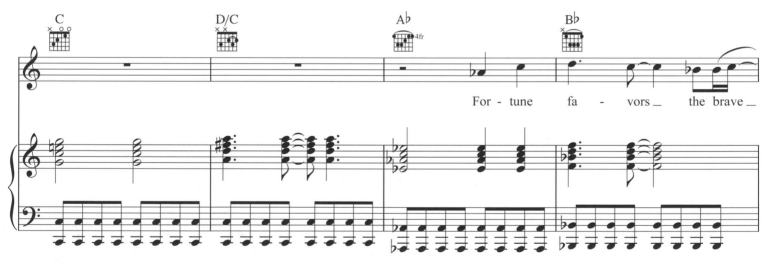

For - tune fa - vors ___ the brave ___

It's all worked ___ out, my

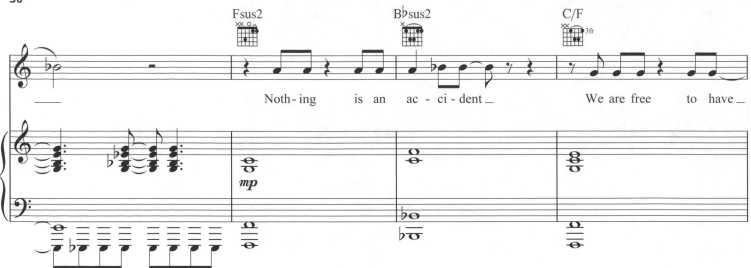

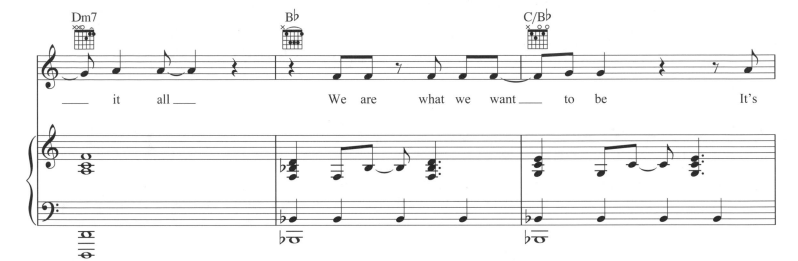

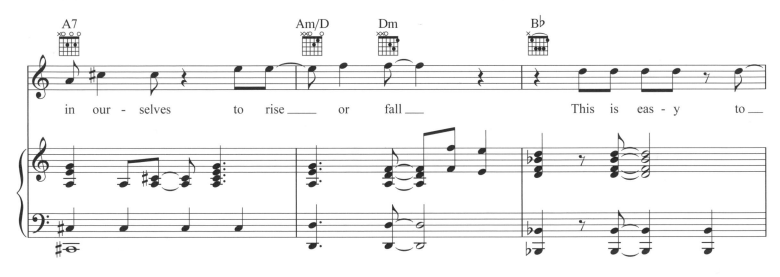

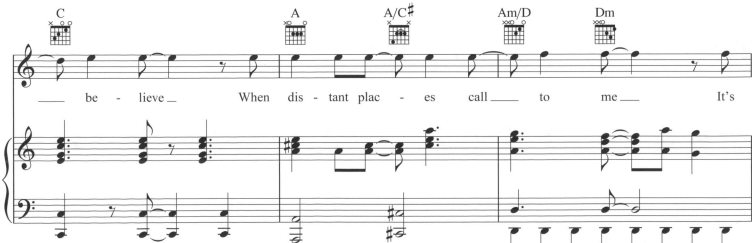

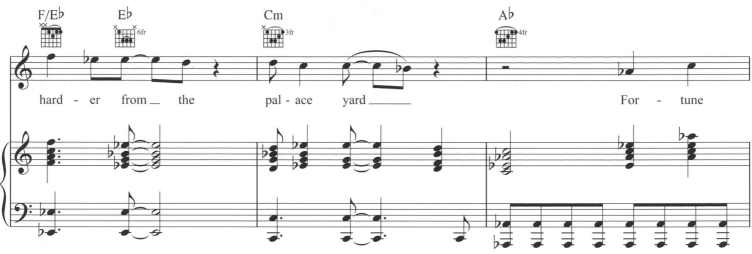

hard - er from __ the pal - ace yard _____ For - tune

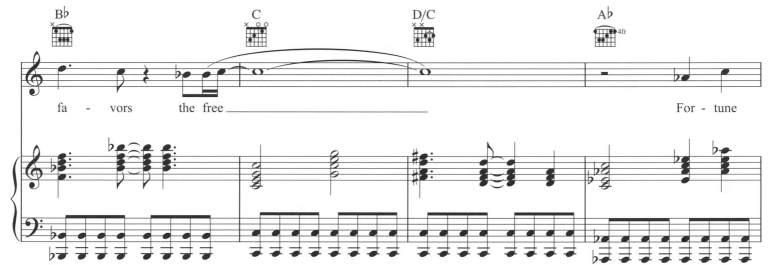

fa - vors the free _____ For - tune

fa - vors the young _____

For - tune fa - vors the brave _____

GOLD
from the Broadway Musical ONCE

Words and Music by
FERGUS O'FARRELL

Moderately, in 1

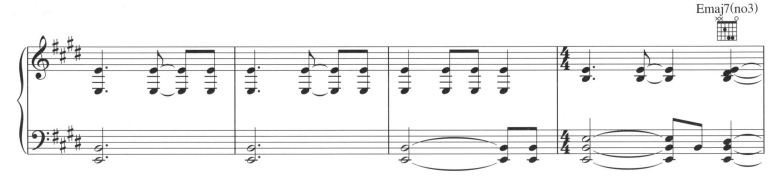

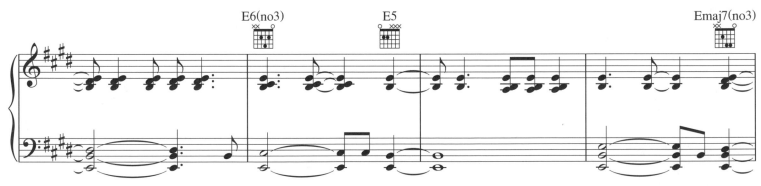

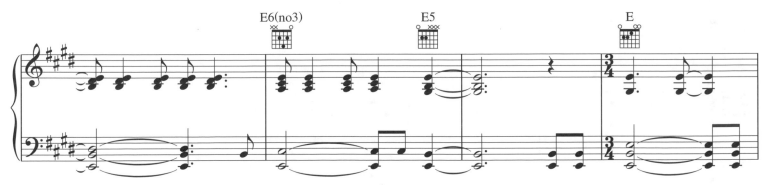

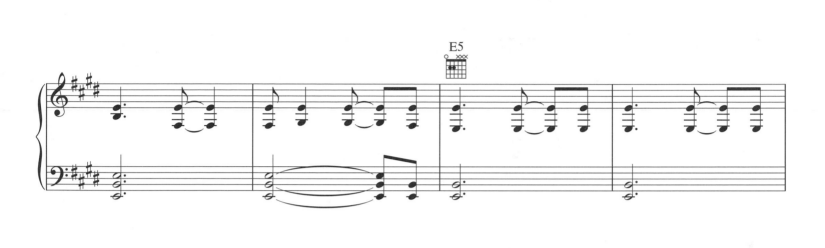

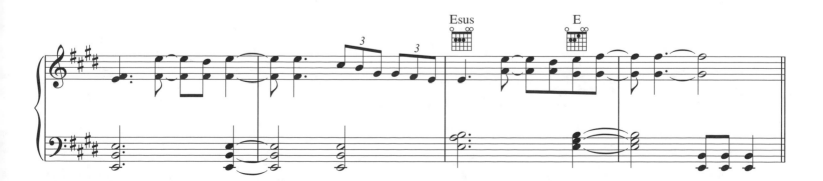

41

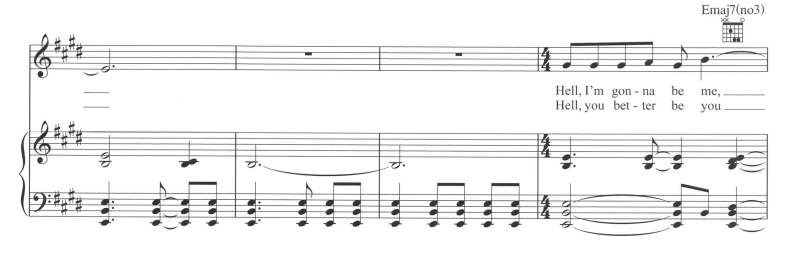

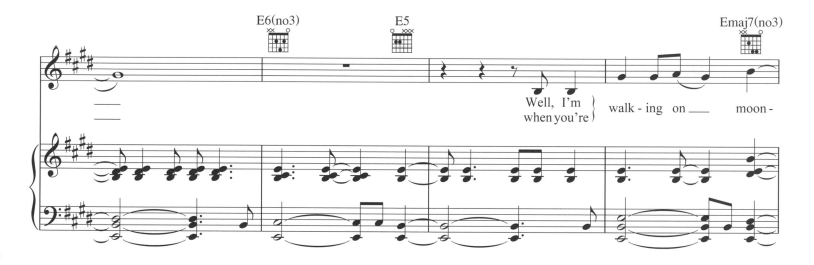

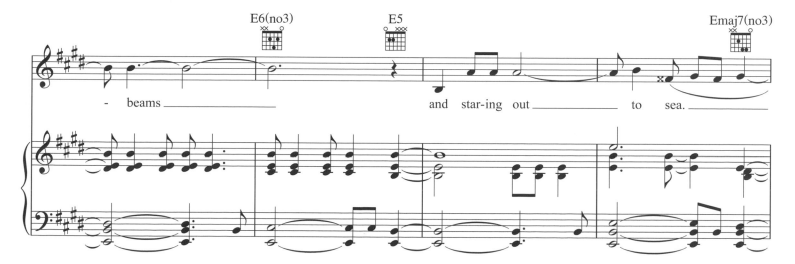

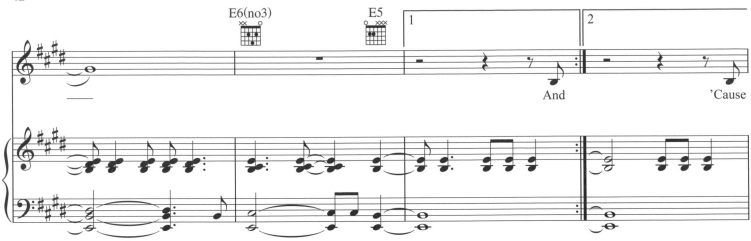

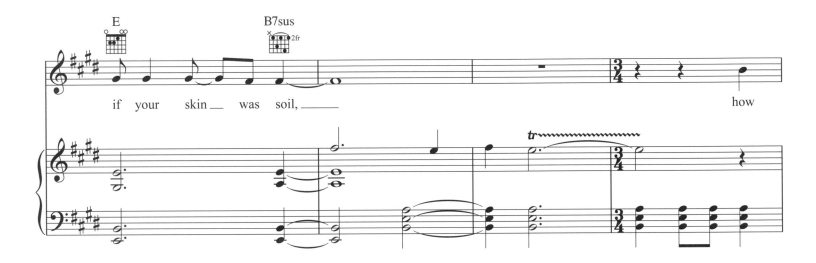

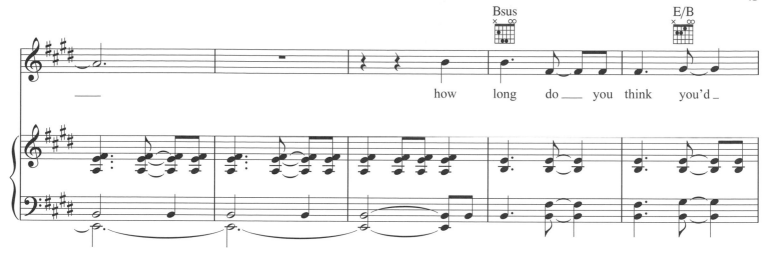

how long do ___ you think you'd ___

stay _____ liv - ing? _____

And I love __ her so; ____

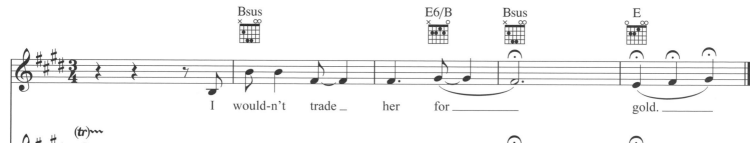

I would-n't trade __ her for _____ gold. _____

HARD TO BE THE BARD
from SOMETHING ROTTEN!

Words and Music by WAYNE KIRKPATRICK
and KAREY KIRKPATRICK

pose for a por-trait, and how I de-plore sit-ting there for e-ter-ni-ty.___ Then it's

off to the inn, where my inn-keep-er friend wants to name a drink af-ter me! Then it's

C9

back to my room, where I re-sume___ my at-tempt to write a hit.___ Just

me and my beer and the ter-ri-ble fear that ____ I might be los-ing it. And it's

SHAKESPEARE:

hard, it's hard. It's real-ly, real-ly hard! ____ So

MANSERVANTS:

It's hard, it's hard. It's real-ly hard! ____

ver-y, ver-y hard. ____ I make it look eas-y, but hon-ey, be-lieve me, it's

Ver-y, ver-y hard. ____

SHAKESPEARE: *Honestly, I don't know how I do it.*
I mean, there's only so much of me that can go around.

un - a - void - a - bly, un - en - joy - a - bly hard. _____ It's hard to be the Bard!

un - a - void - a - bly, un - en - joy - a - bly hard.

SHAKESPEARE: *I know writing made me famous,*
but being famous is just so much more fun.

Play 4 times
(last X)

What peo - ple just don't un - der - stand is that writ - ing's de -

mand - ing, it's men - tal - ly chal - leng - ing, and it's a bore! It's such a chore to sit in a

I BELIEVE
from the Broadway Musical THE BOOK OF MORMON

Words and Music by TREY PARKER,
ROBERT LOPEZ and MATT STONE

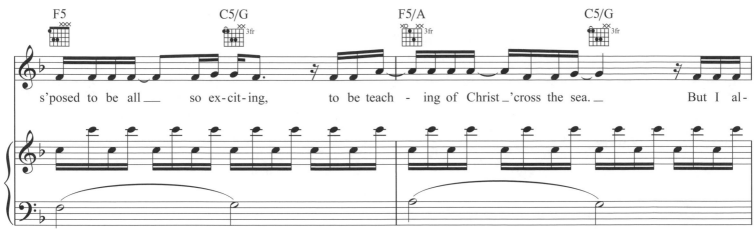

s'posed to be all ___ so ex-cit-ing, to be teach - ing of Christ _'cross the sea. ___ But I al-

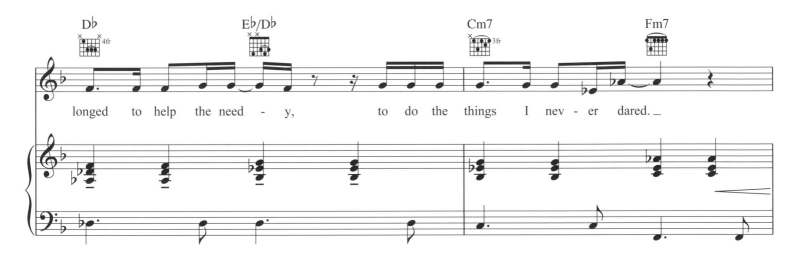

lowed my faith to be shak - en. Oh, what's the mat-ter with me? I've al-ways

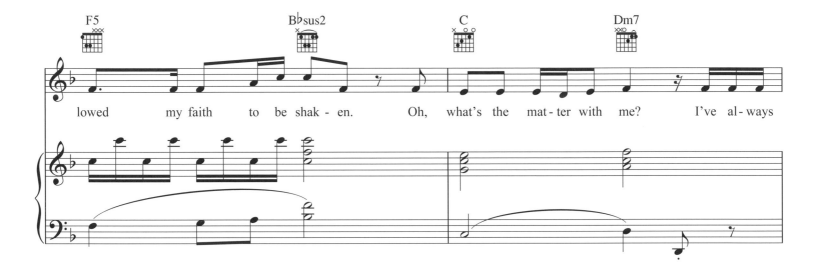

longed to help the need - y, to do the things I nev - er dared. ___

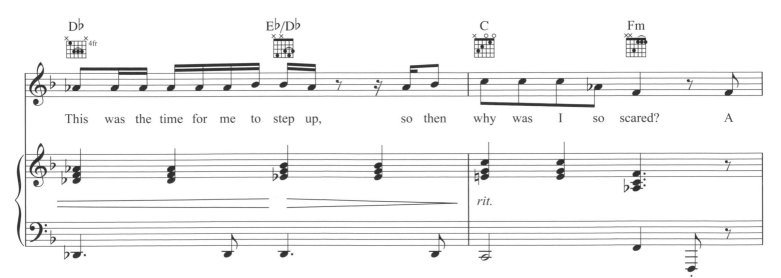

This was the time for me to step up, so then why was I so scared? A

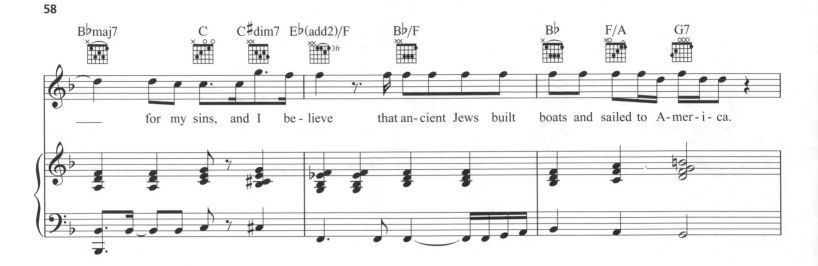

for my sins, and I be-lieve that an-cient Jews built boats and sailed to A-mer-i-ca.

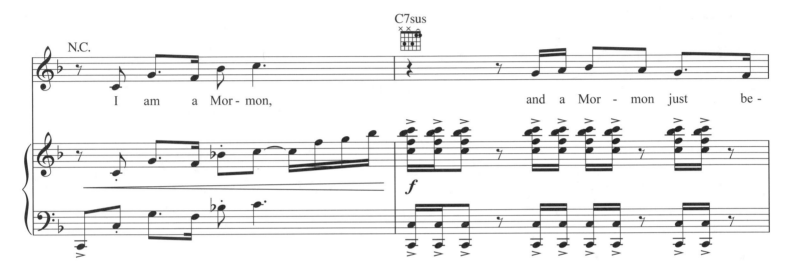

I am a Mor-mon, and a Mor-mon just be-

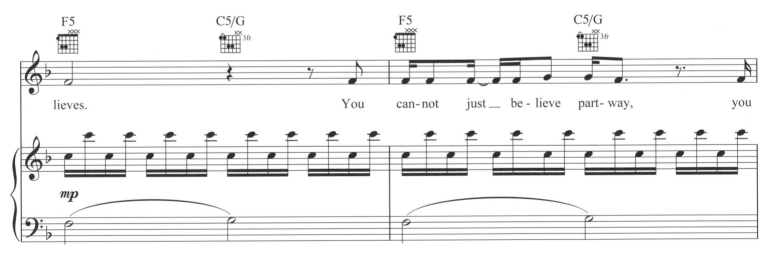

lieves. You can-not just __ be-lieve part-way, you

have to be-lieve __ in it all. __ My prob-lem was doubt-ing the Lord's will in-

me get-ting my own plan-et. And I be-lieve that the cur-rent pres-i-dent of the church, Thom-as

Mon-son, speaks di-rect-ly to God. _ I am a Mor-mon, and,

dang it, a Mor-mon just be-lieves. I

know that I must go and do the things my God com-mands. I

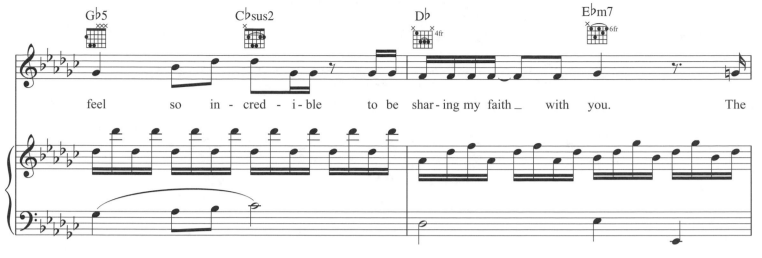

feel so in-cred-i-ble to be shar-ing my faith __ with you. The

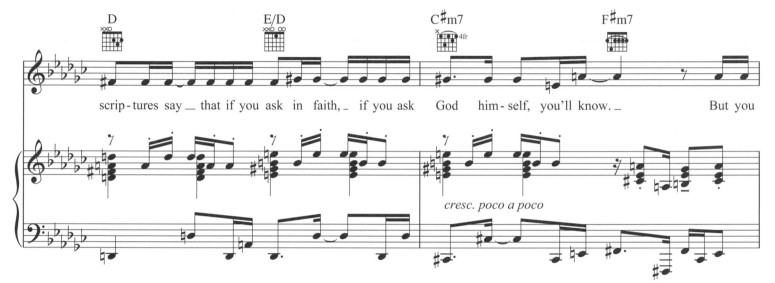

scrip-tures say __ that if you ask in faith, __ if you ask God him-self, you'll know. __ But you

must ask him with-out __ an-y doubt and let your spir-it

grow. I be-lieve _____ that

HER VOICE

from THE LITTLE MERMAID - A BROADWAY MUSICAL

Music by ALAN MENKEN
Lyrics by GLENN SLATER

ERIC:
Where did she go? Where can she be? When will she come a-gain, call-ing to me, call-ing to me, call-ing to me?

Some-where there's a girl who's like the shim-mer of the wind up-on the

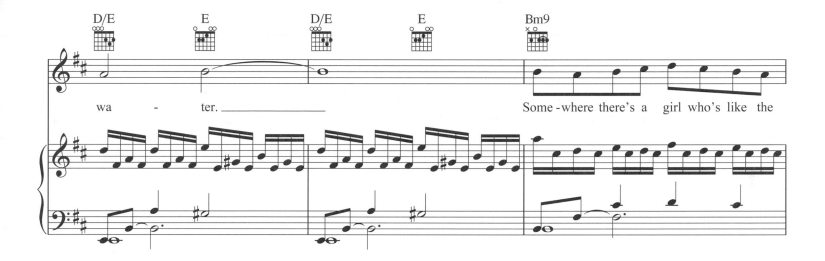

wa - ter. _____ Some-where there's a girl who's like the

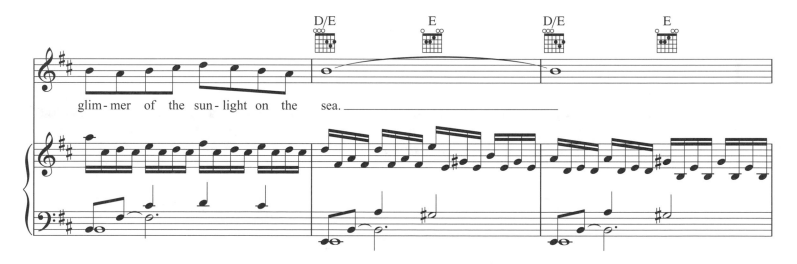

glim-mer of the sun-light on the sea. _____

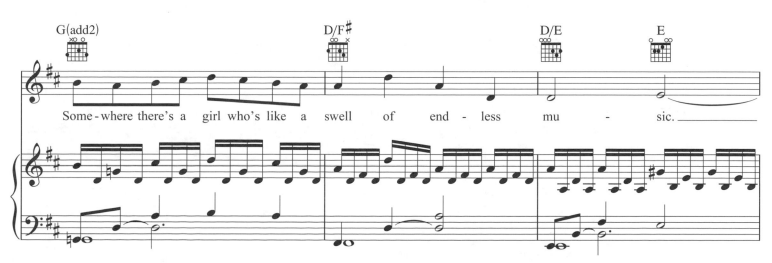

Some-where there's a girl who's like a swell of end-less mu - sic. _____

Some-where she is sing-ing and her song is meant for

me. _____ And her voice, it's

sweet as an-gel's sigh - ing. _____ And her

voice, it's warm as sum - mer sky. _____

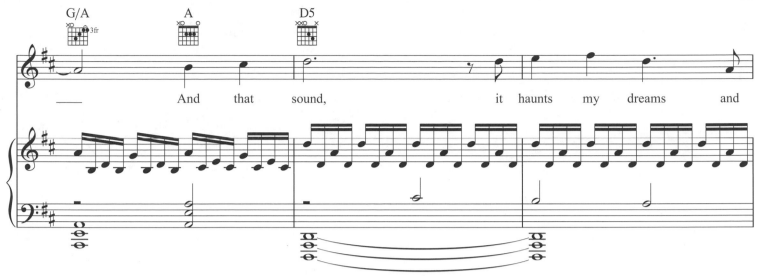

And that sound, it haunts my dreams and

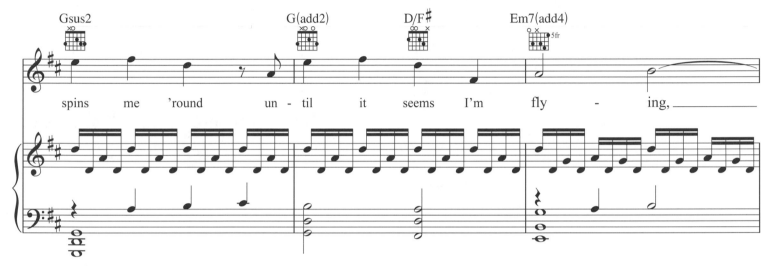

spins me 'round un - til it seems I'm fly - ing, _____

_____ her voice.

I can sense her laugh-ter in the

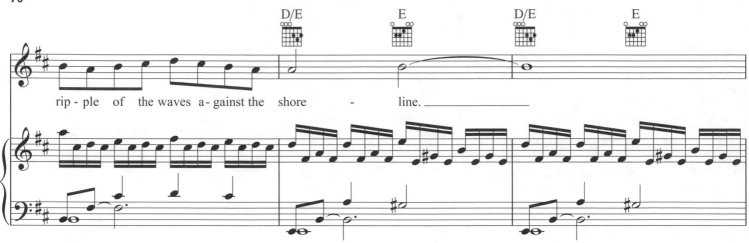

rip - ple of the waves a - gainst the shore - line.

I can see her smil - ing in the moon - light as it set - tles on the sand.

I can feel her wait - ing just be - yond the pale ho -

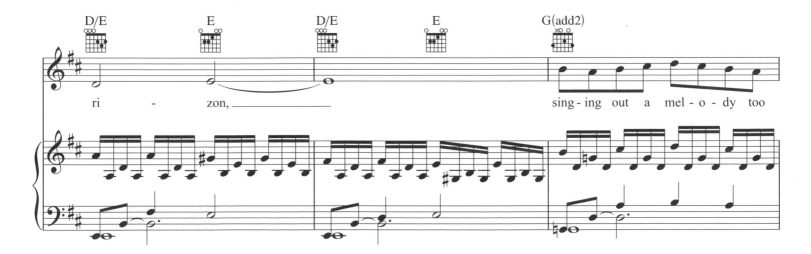

ri - zon, sing - ing out a mel - o - dy too

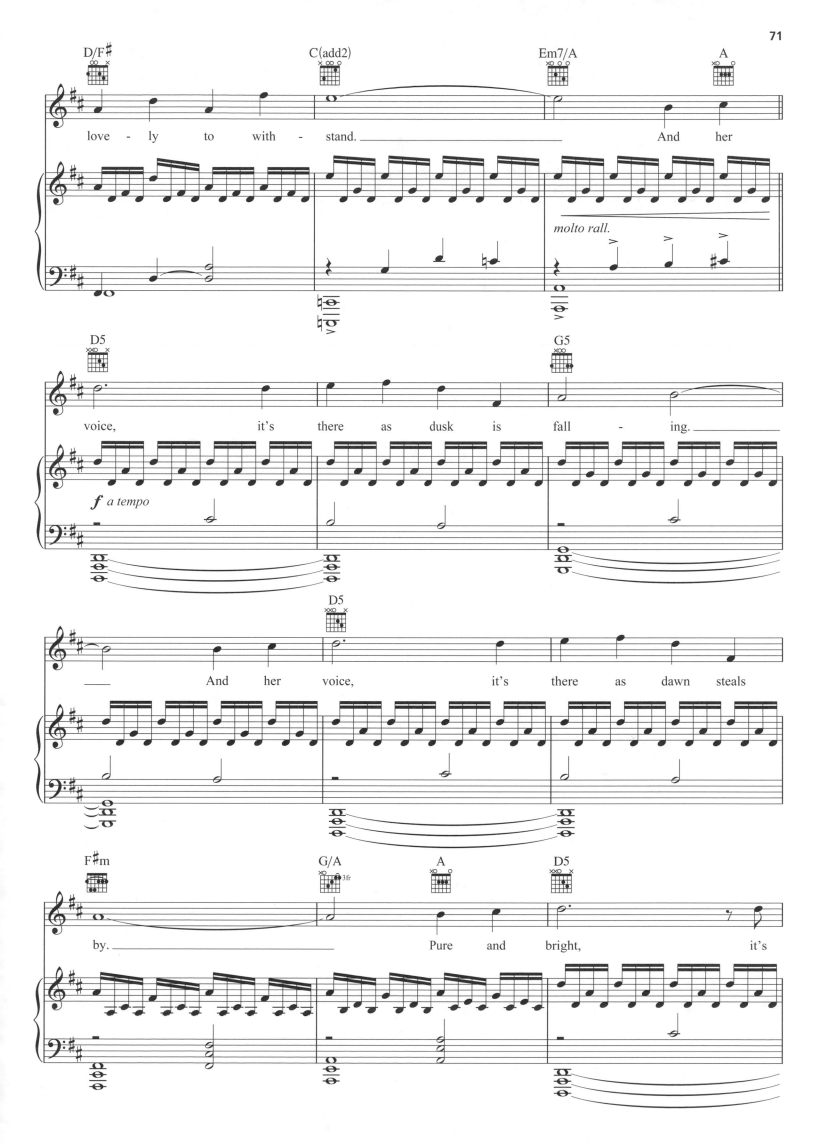

al - ways near. All day, all night, and still I hear it call - ing, _____ her voice. _____

Più mosso

Meno mosso, poco rubato

Strange as a dream,

real as the sea. If you can hear me now, ___ come set me free, ___

come set me free! ___

I AM ALDOLPHO
from THE DROWSY CHAPERONE

Words and Music by LISA LAMBERT
and GREG MORRISON

sure that you have heard the name Al - dol - pho, a la - dies' man who wins ac- claim, Al -

I'M NOT WEARING UNDERWEAR TODAY

from the Broadway Musical AVENUE Q

Music and Lyrics by ROBERT LOPEZ
and JEFF MARX

IF YOU WERE GAY

from the Broadway Musical AVENUE Q

Music and Lyrics by ROBERT LOPEZ
and JEFF MARX

you ___ would ac-cept me, too. ___ If I told

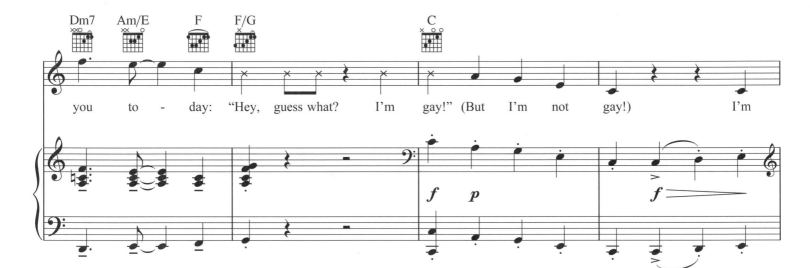

you to - day: "Hey, guess what? I'm gay!" (But I'm not gay!) I'm

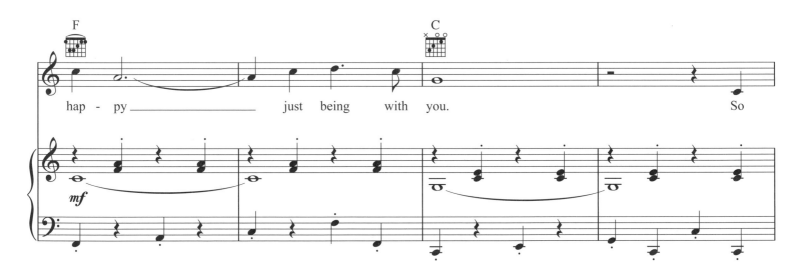

hap - py _____ just being with you. So

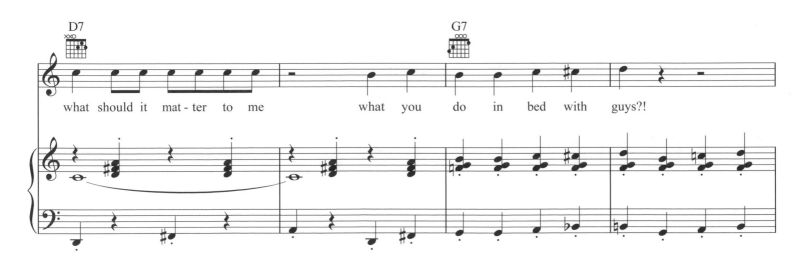

what should it mat - ter to me what you do in bed with guys?!

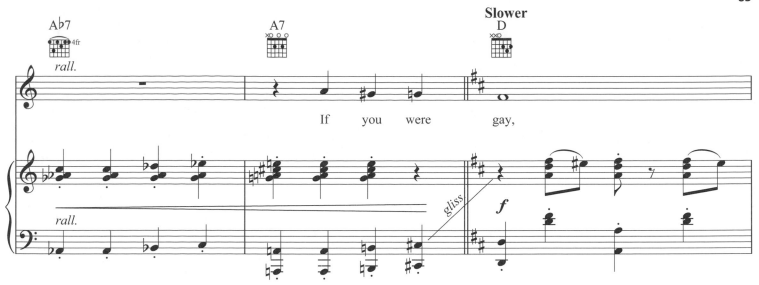

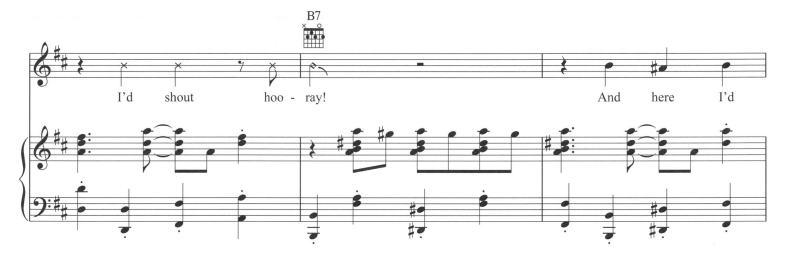

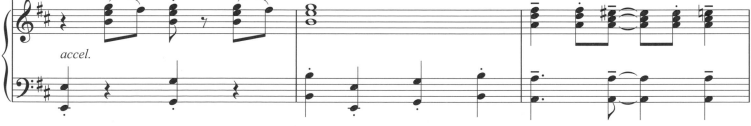

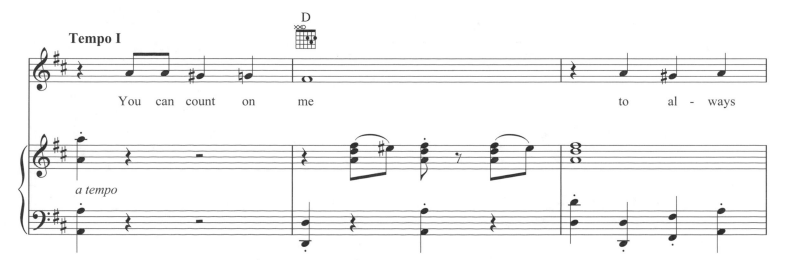

MAN
from THE FULL MONTY

Words and Music by
DAVID YAZBEK

Steady

8vb throughout

You're out of work. Your pride is miss-in'. They call you jerk but you don't lis-ten. You have-n't got a pot to piss in but you're a... man. Your hands are rough. Your back is hair-y. Your talk is

loco

8vb throughout

* air guitar this Led Zeppelin lick

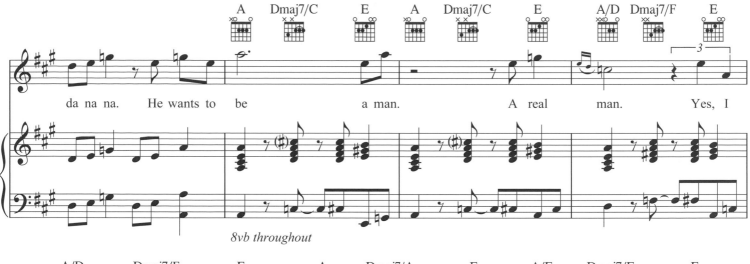

da na na. He wants to be   a man.   A real   man.   Yes, I

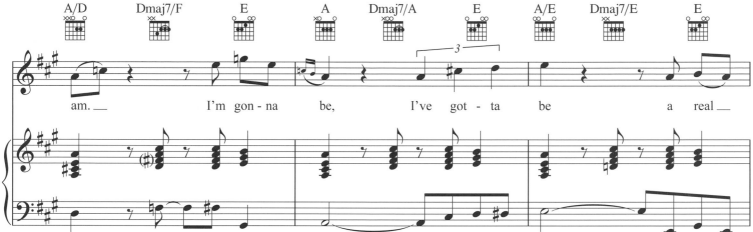

am. ___   I'm gon-na   be,   I've got-ta   be   a real ___

man with a mis-sion like you   see on tel-e-vi-sion. I'm a   real   fine, gen-u-ine ___

man. ___

LEAVE
from the Broadway Musical ONCE

Words and Music by
GLEN HANSARD

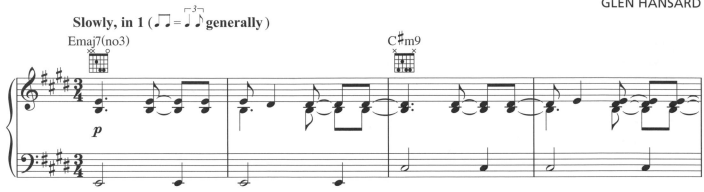

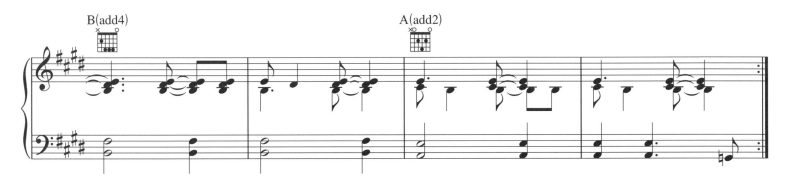

"I can't wait for-ev-er," is
And I hope you feel bet-ter,

all that you said __ be - fore you stood up.
now that it's out. __ What took you so long? _

free your-self; ___ at the same time. ___ Leave,
please your-self; ___ at the same time. ___ Leave,

leave. ___ I don't un - der - stand, ___
leave. ___ Let go of ___ my hand; ___

___ you've al - read - y gone. ___ said what you ___
___ you

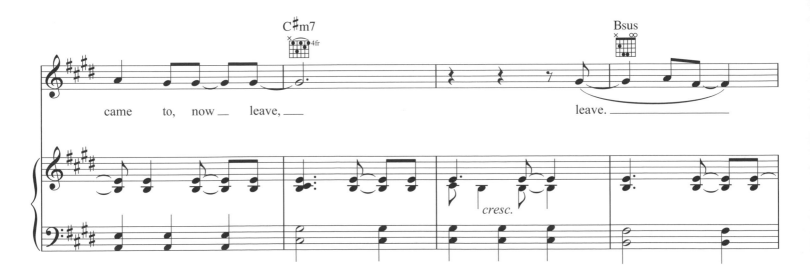

came to, now ___ leave, ___ leave. ___

*Pronounced "eye"

MEMPHIS LIVES IN ME

from MEMPHIS

Music by DAVID BRYAN
Lyrics by JOE DiPIETRO and DAVID BRYAN

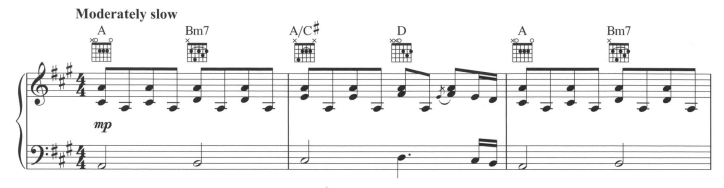

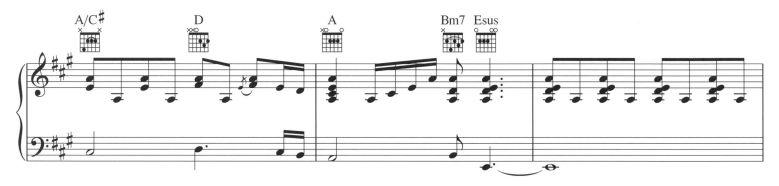

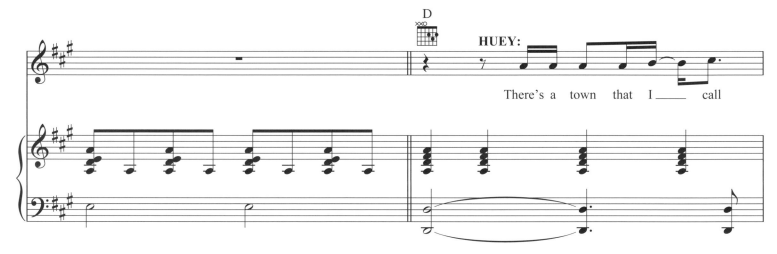

HUEY:

There's a town that I ____ call

home, ____ where all ____ the streets ____ are paved ____ with soul. ____

Down on Beale there's a hon-ky-tonk bar.

Hear the wail of a blues gui-tar. Have a beer and drop a dime in the blind man's

jar.

The blues sing soft-ly in the air, like a Sun-day morn-ing prayer.

PROUD OF YOUR BOY

from ALADDIN

Music by ALAN MENKEN
Lyrics by HOWARD ASHMAN

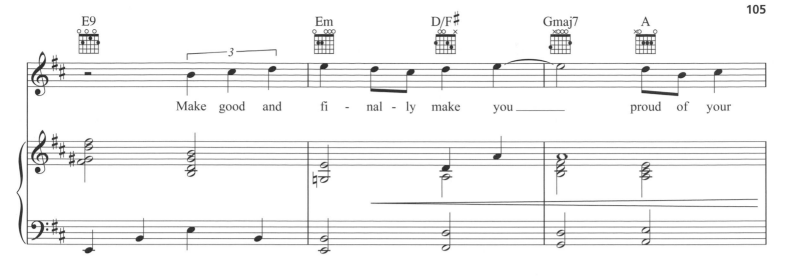

Make good and fi - nal - ly make you _____ proud of your

Moving forward

boy! _____

Poco più mosso

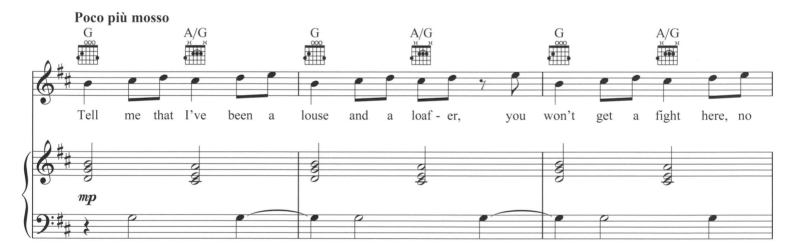

Tell me that I've been a louse and a loaf - er, you won't get a fight here, no

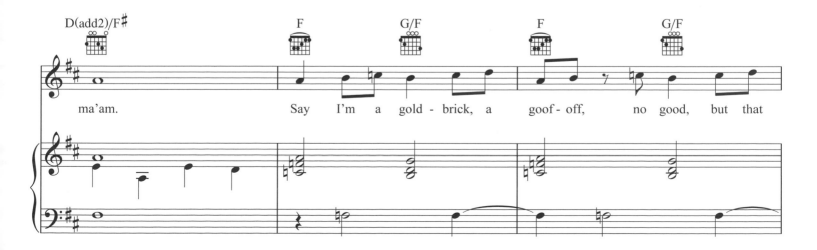

ma'am. Say I'm a gold - brick, a goof - off, no good, but that

MY UNFORTUNATE ERECTION

from THE 25TH ANNUAL PUTNAM COUNTY SPELLING BEE

Words and Music by
WILLIAM FINN

SANTA FE
from NEWSIES THE MUSICAL

Music by ALAN MENKEN
Lyrics by JACK FELDMAN

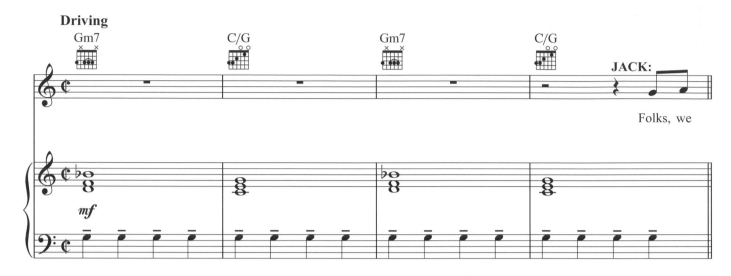

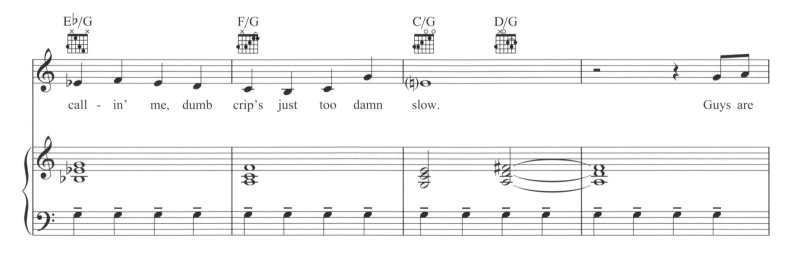

Why should you on-ly take what you're giv-en? Why should you spend your whole life liv-in' trapped where there ain't no fu-ture, e-ven at sev-en-teen, break-in' your back for some-one else-'s sake? If the life don't seem to suit ya, how 'bout a change of

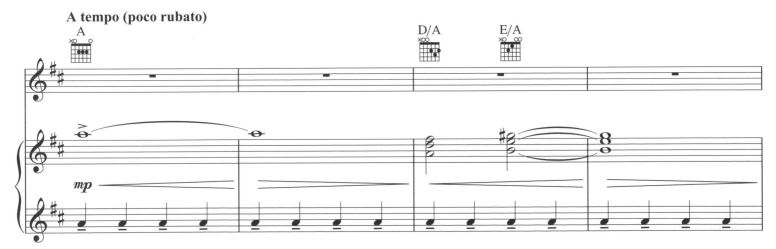

Just be real is all I'm ask-in', not some

paint-in' in my head. 'Cause I'm dead if I can't count on you to-

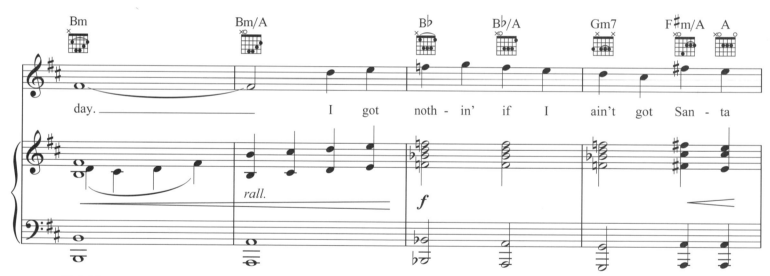

day._____ I got noth-in' if I ain't got San-ta

Briskly

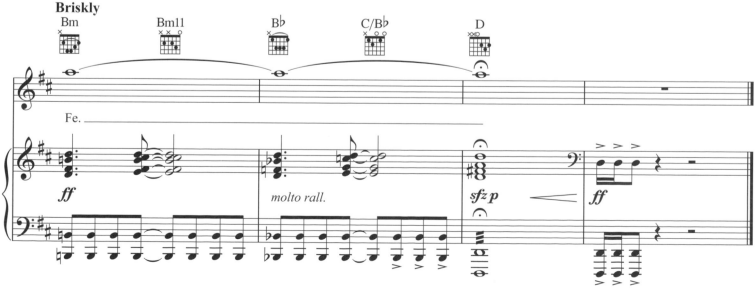

Fe._____

SAY IT TO ME NOW

from the Broadway Musical ONCE

Words and Music by GLEN HANSARD,
GRAHAM DOWNEY, PAUL BRENNAN,
NOREEN O'DONNELL, COLM MACCONIOMAIRE
and DAVID ODLUM

Moderately slow

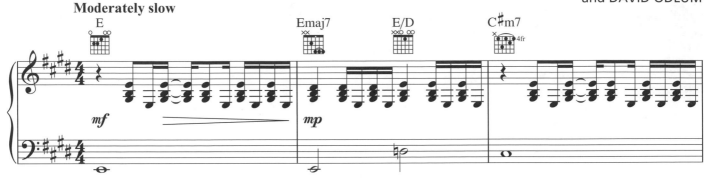

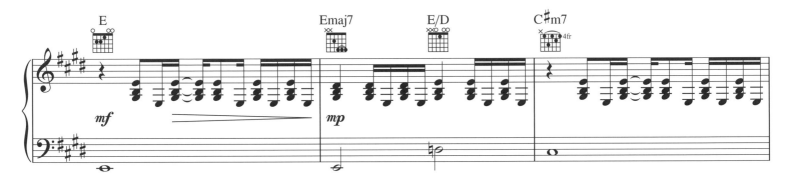

GUY:
Scratch-ing at the sur-face now;

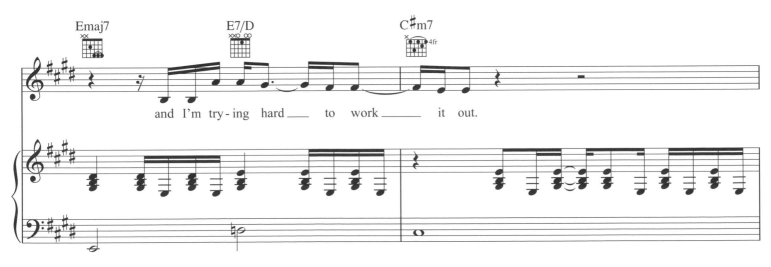

and I'm try-ing hard ___ to work ___ it out.

And so much has gone mis-un-der-stood, __

and this mys-t'ry on - ly leads ____ to doubt.

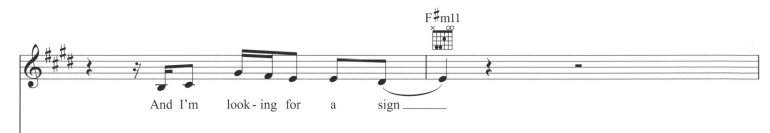

And I'm look-ing for a sign ____

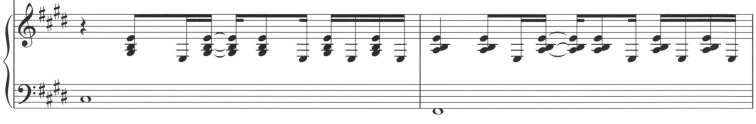

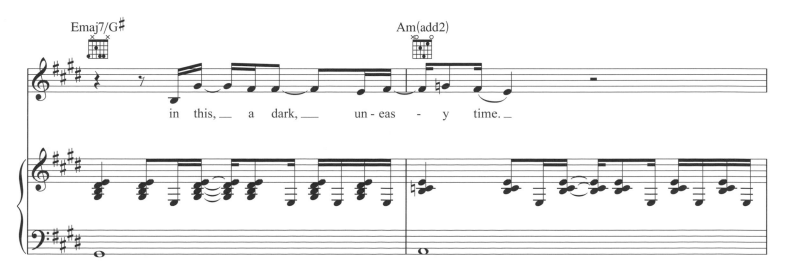

in this, __ a dark, __ un-eas - y time. __

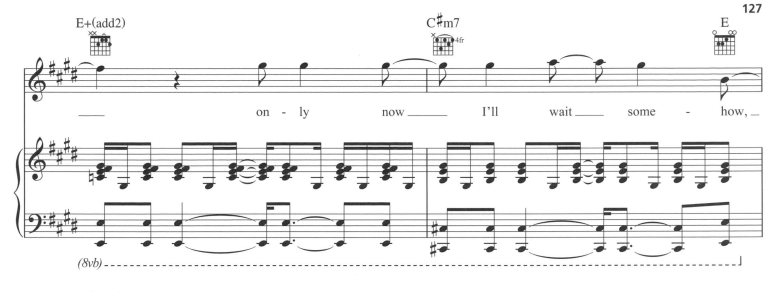

on - ly now _____ I'll wait _____ some - how, _____

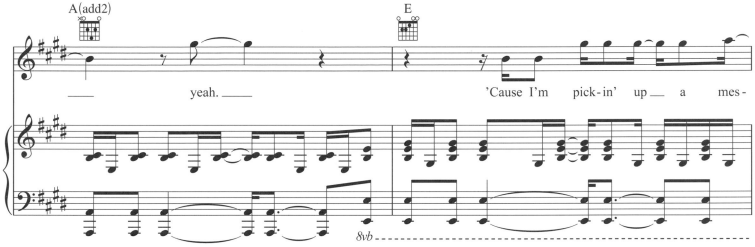

_____ yeah. _____ 'Cause I'm pick - in' up _____ a mes -

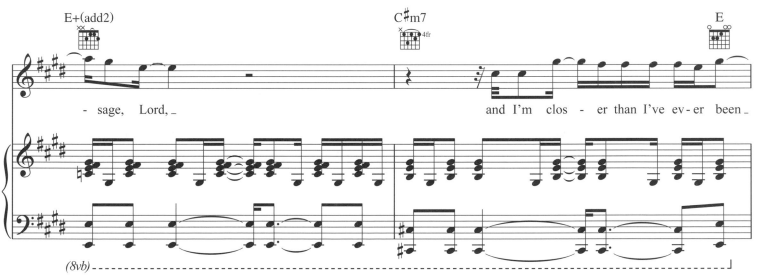

- sage, Lord, _ and I'm clos - er than I've ev - er been _

_____ be - fore. _ So if you have _____ some - thing

WAVING THROUGH A WINDOW
from DEAR EVAN HANSEN

Music and Lyrics by BENJ PASEK
and JUSTIN PAUL
Vocal arrangements by Justin Paul
Piano arrangement by
Alex Lacamoire and Justin Paul

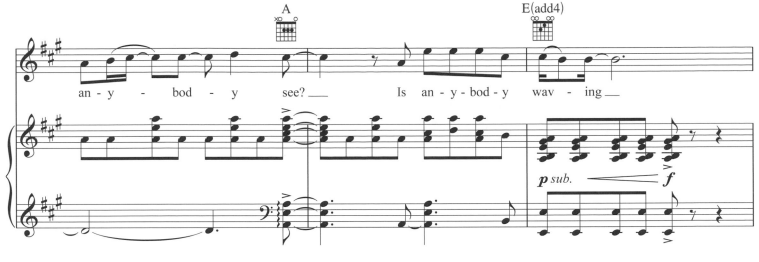

an-y-bod-y see? __ Is an-y-bod-y wav - ing __

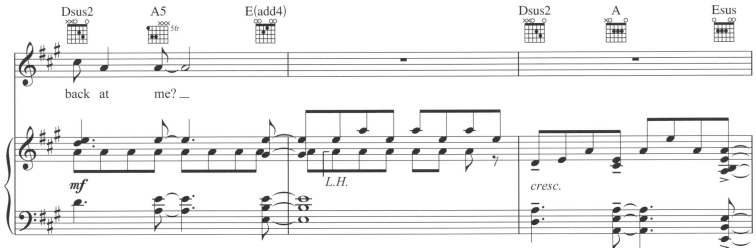

back at me? __

Lift (♩ = 146)

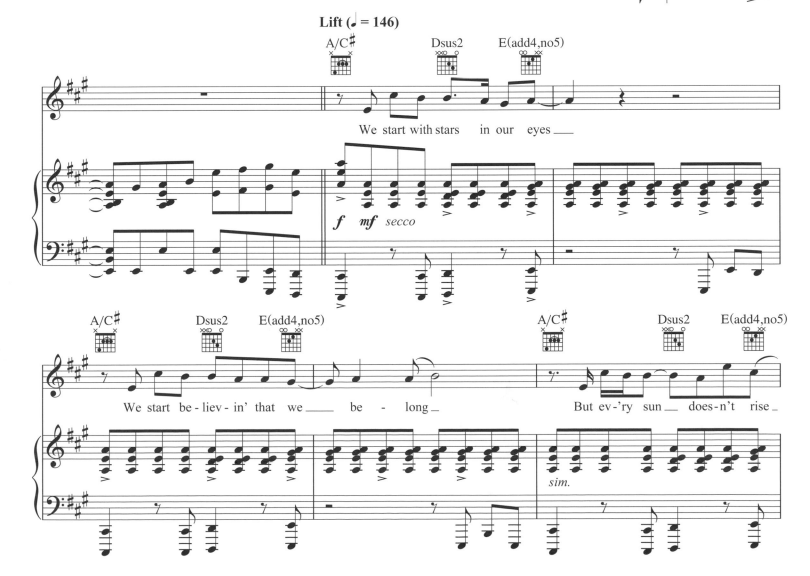

We start with stars in our eyes __

We start be-liev-in' that we __ be - long __ But ev-'ry sun __ does-n't rise __

THE STREETS OF DUBLIN
from A MAN OF NO IMPORTANCE

Words by LYNN AHRENS
Music by STEPHEN FLAHERTY

come with me, you'll know _____ how the

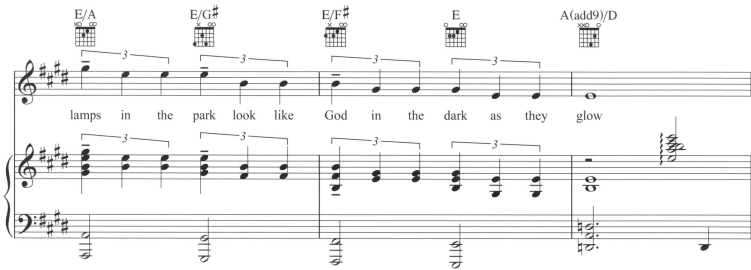

lamps in the park look like God in the dark as they glow

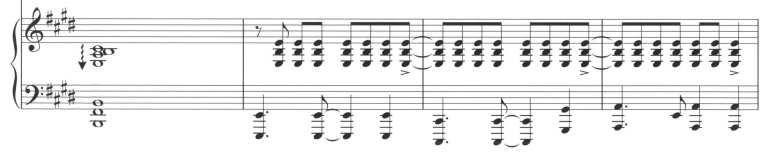

on the streets of Dub - lin. _____

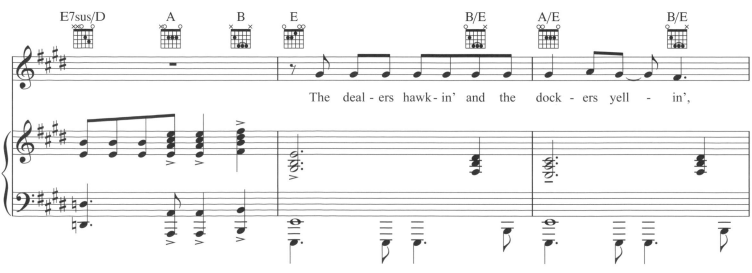

The deal - ers hawk - in' and the dock - ers yell - in',

-lin. _____ And there's mu-sic like noth - in' you've heard _

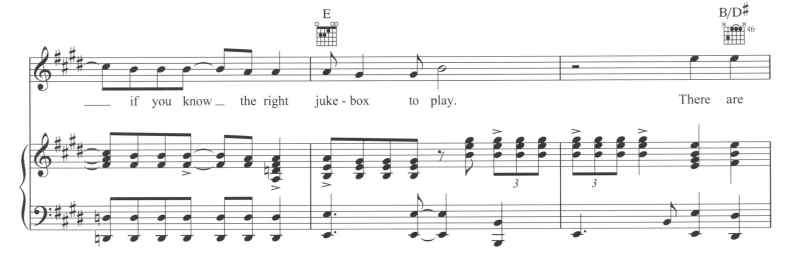

_____ if you know _ the right juke-box to play. There are

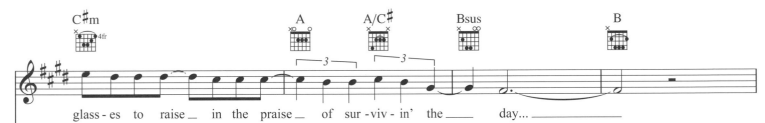

glass - es to raise _ in the praise _ of sur -viv - in' the ____ day... _____

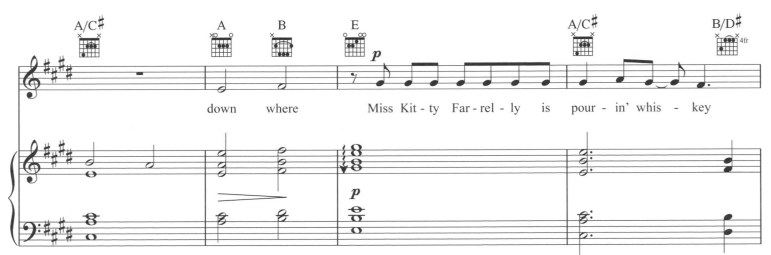

down where Miss Kit-ty Far-rel-ly is pour-in' whis-key

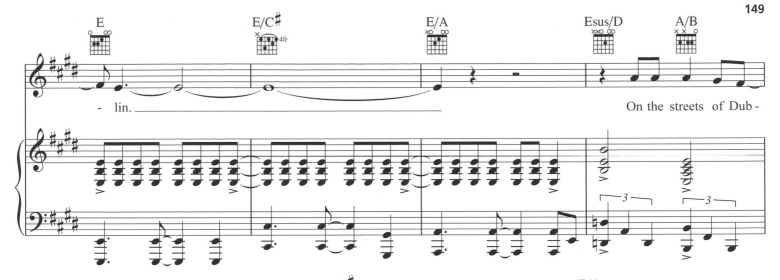

TAKE A CHANCE ON ME

from the Stage Musical LITTLE WOMEN

Music by JASON HOWLAND
Lyrics by MINDI DICKSTEIN

This is ver-y nice, such a love-ly par-ty. The mu-sic sounds so thrill-ing. ____

____ It makes a per-son feel like danc - ing. ____

(rhythmically steady)

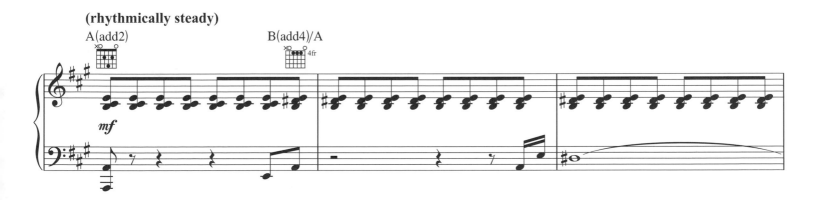

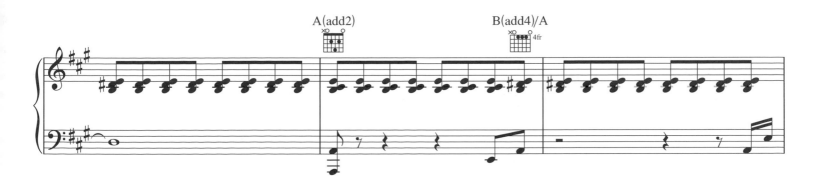

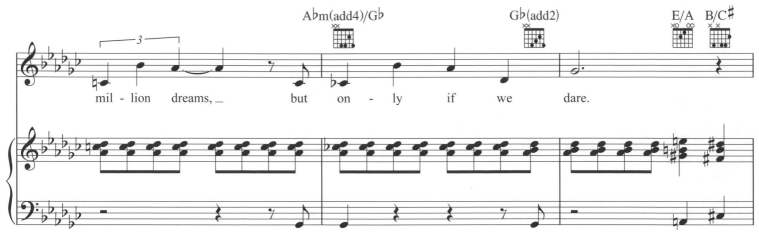

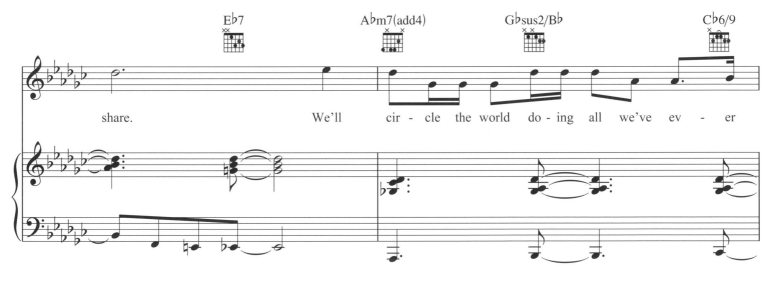

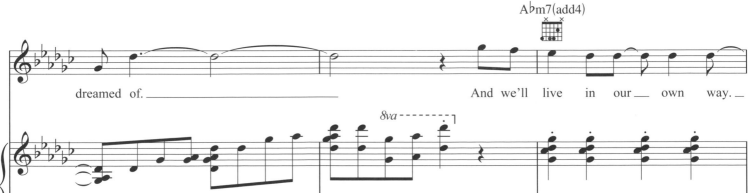

WHAT DO I NEED WITH LOVE

from THOROUGHLY MODERN MILLIE

Music by JEANINE TESORI
Lyrics by DICK SCANLAN

Freely, conversational

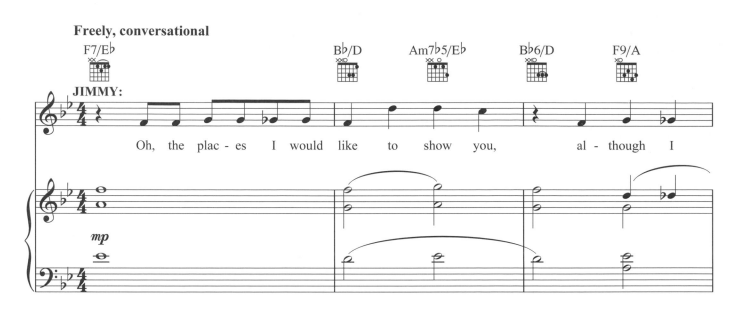

JIMMY:
Oh, the plac-es I would like to show you, al-though I

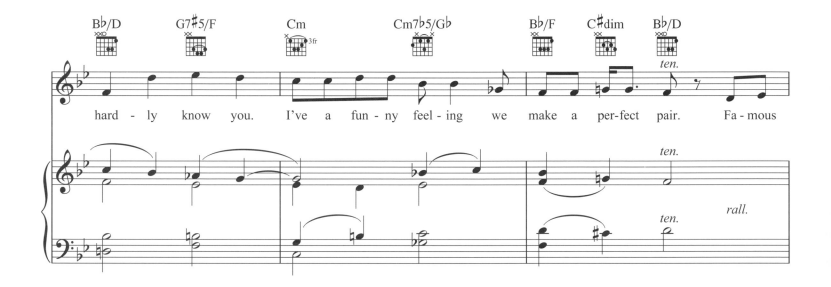

hard-ly know you. I've a fun-ny feel-ing we make a per-fect pair. Fa-mous

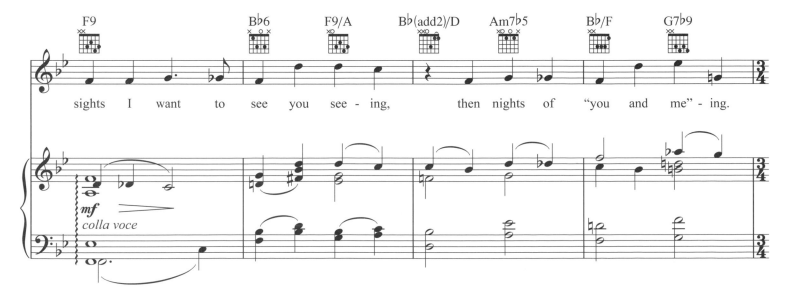

sights I want to see you see-ing, then nights of "you and me"-ing.

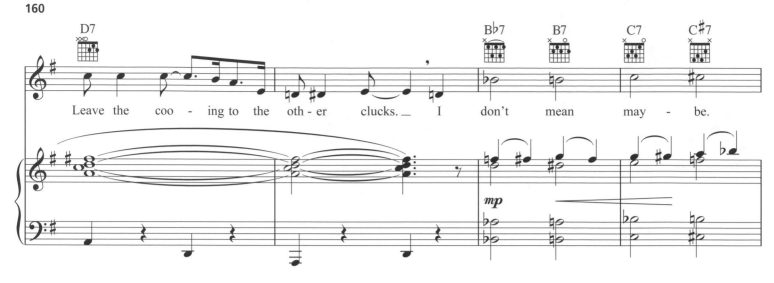

Leave the coo - ing to the oth - er clucks. __ I don't mean may - be.

Got it good. __ What do I need __ with love?

Al - ways prac - tice what I preach: __ keep temp - ta - tion out of eas - y reach. __

Stick to dolls who wash their hair in bleach, __ I'm __ hap - py.

Come and go the way I choose. __ Nev - er gon - na sing the

tied - down blues. __ Oth - er guys __ would kill to fill my shoes. __ No

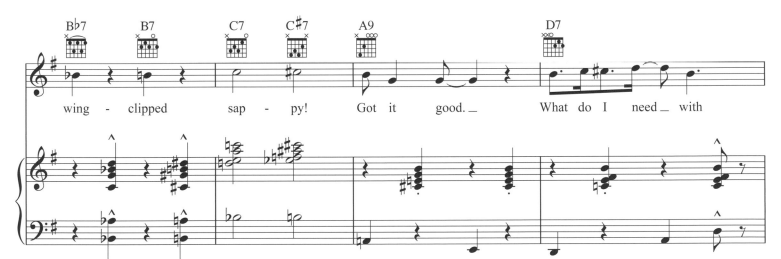

wing - clipped sap - py! Got it good. __ What do I need __ with

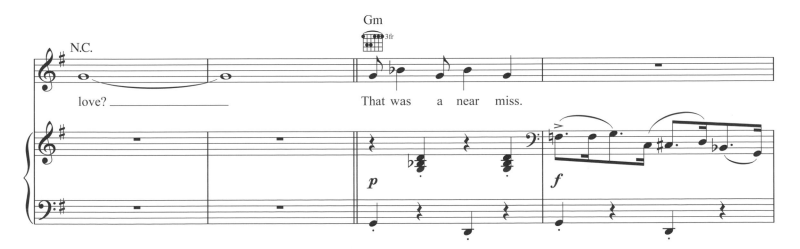

love? _____ That was a near miss.

Got it good. ___ What do I need ___ with love? ___

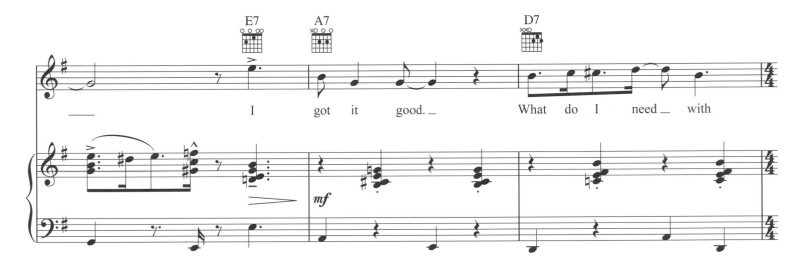

___ I got it good. ___ What do I need ___ with

Double-time feel, straight 8ths

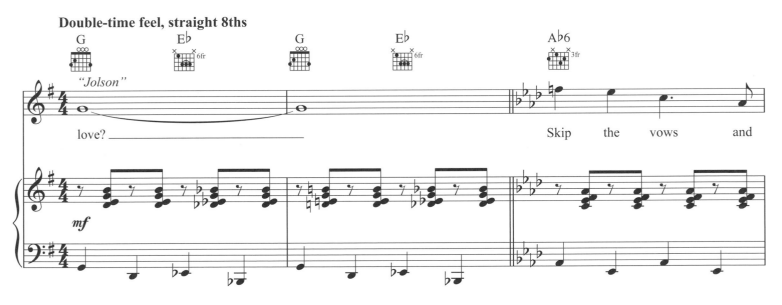

"Jolson"

love? ___ Skip the vows and

all that rot. ___ Tell the min-is-ter that "I ___ do" ___ not.

got it good. __

Got it good. _____ I got it

bad! _____

WHAT IS IT ABOUT HER?

from THE WILD PARTY

Music and Lyrics by
ANDREW LIPPA

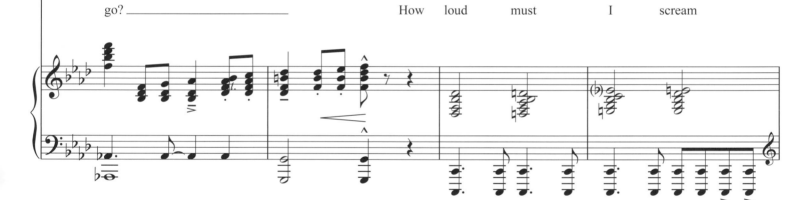

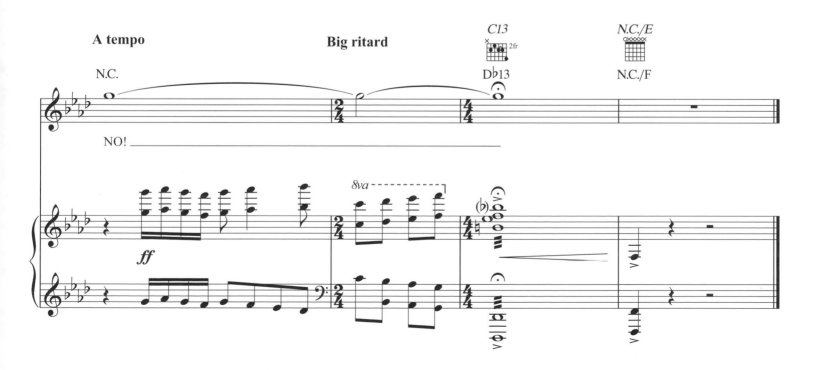

WHEN WORDS FAIL
from SHREK THE MUSICAL

Words and Music by JEANINE TESORI
and DAVID LINDSAY-ABAIRE

With a wee lilt

SHREK:

Spoken: Princess, I... How's it goin', first of all?
Good? And for me too, I'm okay... um...

I picked this flow-er; ___

right o-ver there is where it grew. And I don't real-ly

like it, but it made me think of you, be-cause it's pret-ty, ___ is

what I'm try'n' to say. And you are al - so pret - ty, but I like you

an - y - way. So please ac - cept this flow - er with its

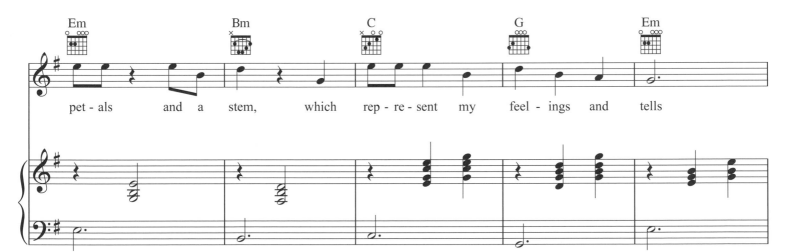

pet - als and a stem, which rep - re - sent my feel - ings and tells

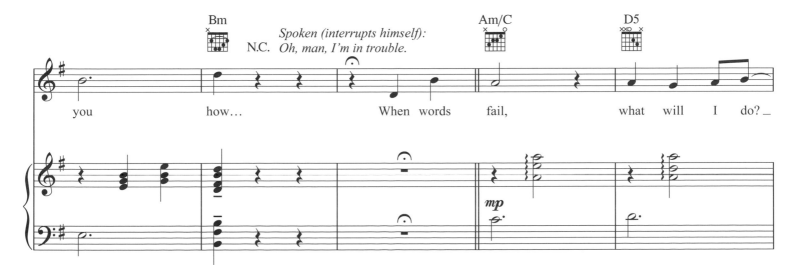

you how... *Spoken (interrupts himself): Oh, man, I'm in trouble.* When words fail, what will I do? _

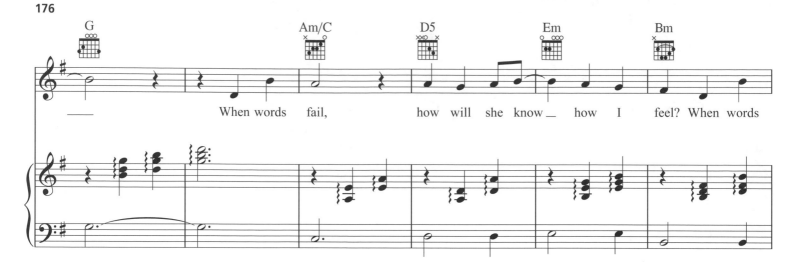

When words fail, how will she know ___ how I feel? When words

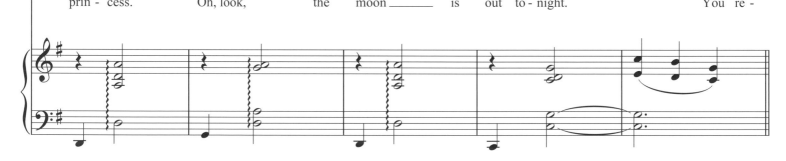

fail, will I fail ___ too? ___ Hel - lo, ___ fair

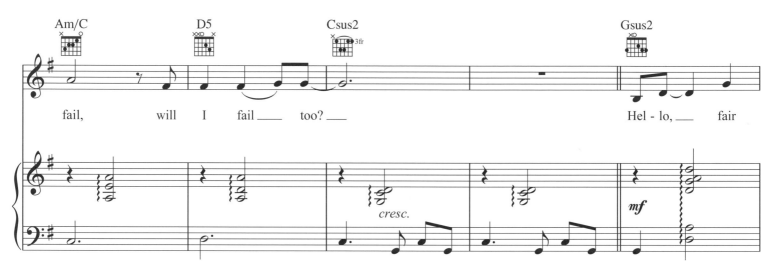

prin - cess. Oh, look, the moon ___ is out to - night. You re -

mind me of that moon be - cause it's big and bright; and by big, I don't mean

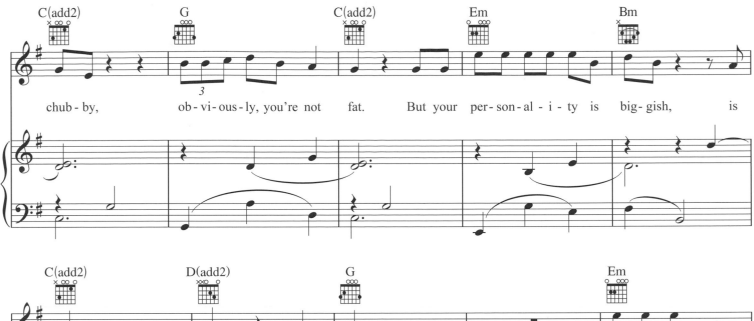

chub-by, ob-vi-ous-ly, you're not fat. But your per-son-al-i-ty is big-gish, is

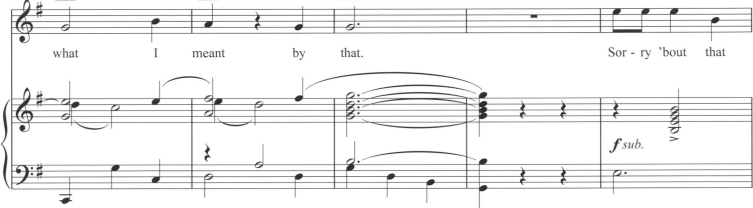

what I meant by that. Sor-ry 'bout that

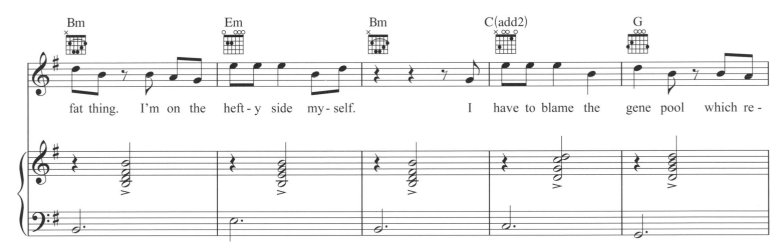

fat thing. I'm on the heft-y side my-self. I have to blame the gene pool which re-

Spoken: Oh, where am I going with this?

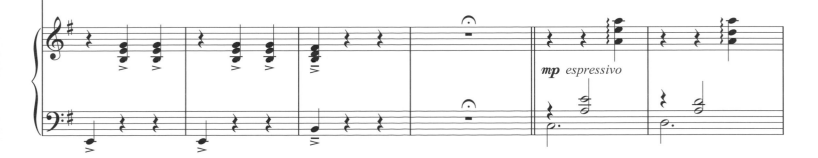

minds me of... When words fail, what will I do? _

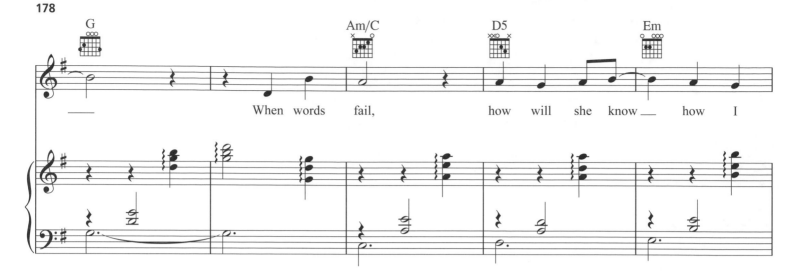

When words fail, how will she know ___ how I

feel? When words fail, will I fail ___ too? ___ Do I have a

snow-ball's chance? ___ Are my pros-pects just too grim? ___ I

spent my life stuck in the mud. ___ Now I'm crawl-ing out on a limb. ___

WHEN YOUR MIND'S MADE UP

from the Broadway Musical ONCE

Words and Music by
GLEN HANSARD

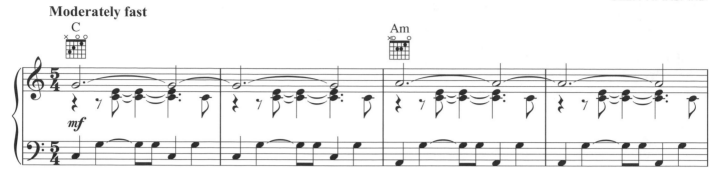

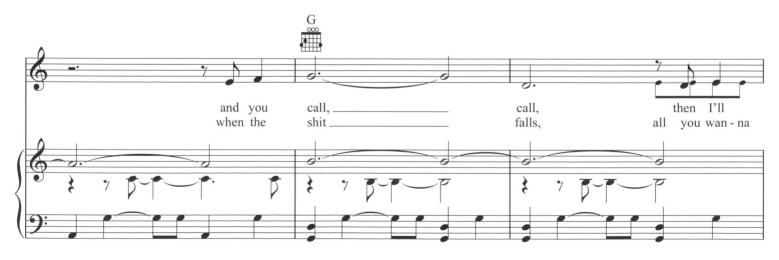

come run - ning _____ to fight. _____
do is run _____ a - way _____

And I'll be at your door when there's
and hide all by your- self. On this

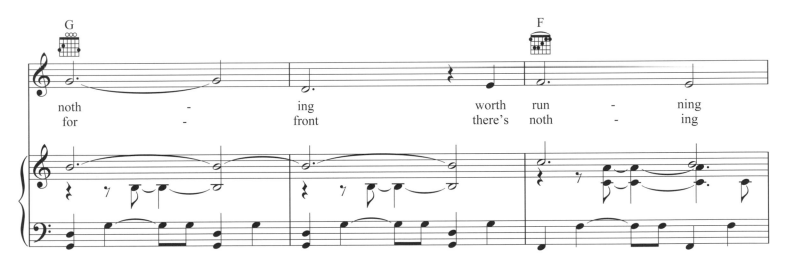

noth - ing worth run - ning
for - front there's noth - ing

for. _____ } When your mind's _____ made up, when your
else. _____ }

mind's _____ made up, _____ there's no point _ try-ing to

change it. ___ When your mind's _____ made up, _____ when your

mind's _____ made up, _____ there's no point _ { try-ing to / e - ven

stop it. ___ You see, _ talk - ing. ___ When your mind's _____ made

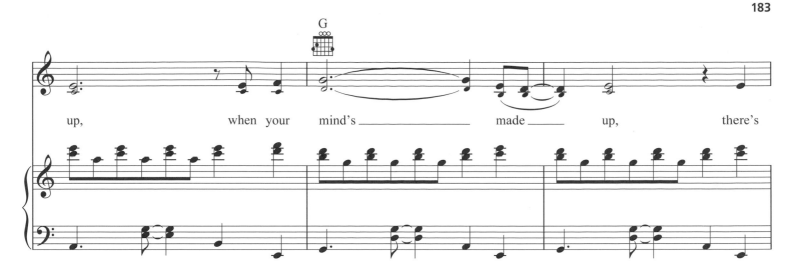

up,   when your mind's _____ made _____ up,   there's

no point _ try-ing to fight it. ___ When your mind's, _____

your mind,... _____

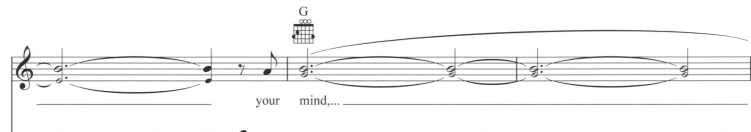

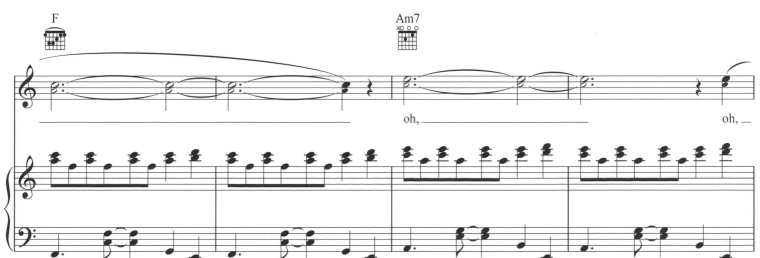

oh, _____   oh, __

there's no point __ try-ing to

change it. So, __ if you ev-er want

some-thing, __ and you call, __

call, then I'll come run - ning. __